Architecture Profile 3
GRAFTON ARCHITECTS

Published as part of Gandon Editions'
PROFILES series on Irish architects
(details page 59).

ISBN 0946846 057

Editor   John O'Regan

Asst Editor   Nicola Dearey
Design   John O'Regan (© 1999)
Production   Gandon Editions

Printing   Nicholson & Bass, Belfast

Distributed by Gandon and its overseas agents

GANDON EDITIONS
Oysterhaven, Kinsale, Co Cork, Ireland

tel   +353 (0)21-770830
fax   +353 (0)21-770755
e-mail   gandon@eircom.net
web-site   www.gandon-editions.com

Photography

Dennis Gilbert   cover, 4, 17, 19, 24, 25r,
                  25bl, 32, 33tl, 34, 35, 36, 37,
                  38, 39b, 43, 45tr, 45br, 48,
                  49, 50
                  (© Dennis Gilbert, VIEW)
Bill Hastings   25tl, 44tl, 44bl, 47
Gerry Hayden   line drawings
Kate Horgan   54
Ros Kavanagh   20, 21, 22bl, 22br, 23, 26,
                  29, 44tr, 44br, 45bl, 56
Tim Kovar   18
Ciaran O'Brien   42
John Searle   models, colour drawings

other photographs by the architects

Illustrations

cover   Dept of Mechanical
                Engineering, Trinity College
frontispiece   Eco House
page 58   Civic Centre, Dunshaughlin

Publication grant-aided by
The Arts Council / An Chomhairle Ealaíon
and assisted by
The Royal Institute of the Architects of Ireland

Profile

Grafton Architects

GANDON EDITIONS

At Home in the City

Grafton Architects' Urban Domestic

HUGH CAMPBELL

In his passionate account of modernity, *All that is Solid Melts into Air*, the American writer Marshall Berman describes the role of the rebuilt Nevsky Prospect in nineteenth-century St Petersburg:

> The essential purpose of this street, which gives it its special character, is sociability: people come here to see and be seen, and to communicate their visions to one another, not for any ulterior purpose, without greed or competition, but as an end in itself.[1]

Grafton Street, where Grafton Architects work, has a similar significance in Dublin. This narrow pedestrianised street of shops is central to the the city's civic society. Every week it is thronged with Dubliners of all types, strolling, meeting acquaintances, people-watching. Its meandering route slows people down, hoards them together, encourages communication. This is no mere conduit of traffic or showcase of consumer goods; its significance goes beyond that. Although created by the unsentimental forces of trade and commerce, it has become a space where people can partake of something larger than themselves, can feel part of an urban community. This decidedly urban character also has something peculiarly Irish to it.

Temple Bar Square
Dublin 2 (1992-96)

Although densely crowded, Grafton Street doesn't feel anonymous or threatening. It is invigorating, but at the same time familiar and vaguely comforting. It allows a sense of belonging in and ownership of the city. This sense seems also to underlie a lot of Grafton Architects' recent work, and it is hard to know whether it emerges as a result of their prolonged exposure to the life of the street, or whether their choice of name and location reflects a set of already well-established concerns.

In a series of projects of widely varying scale, Grafton Architects have been investigating ways of living in the city. The time when Dublin was in a perilous state of disuse and dereliction, and when the idea of large numbers of people inhabiting its centre seemed far-fetched, now feels like long ago. The past few years have seen a scramble to fill every vacant corner of the city, to redevelop every vaguely suitable building, to reclaim every previously 'unsavoury' area with new apartments. These apartments sell by the thousand to single people and young couples who want to be near the centre of things, living close to where they work and socialise. This possibility is so much preferable to the damp bedsits in the suburbs that might previously have been the lot of these new urbanites that they are probably indifferent to the relatively poor quality of much of what has been built. It is left for those who had initially championed the cause of urban renewal to bemoan the results of recent feverish development. Careful, considered urban architecture seems a remote possibility. After all, in a market where everything sells, what place is there for the perennial staples of the architect, 'commodity, firmness and delight'? Serious architects are now beginning to grapple with this question, and rather than turn their backs on the world of the developer, they have entered into tentative dialogue.

One of the first fruits of that dialogue is the apartment building which Grafton Architects have designed in Smithfield. This scheme occupies one corner of a busy intersection in a gritty part of the north-west city which has only recently begun to fill with the cranes and hoardings which are the harbingers of large-scale apartment development. Until recently, the architectural input into most such developments has been minimal. Apartments are small and barely functional. Economies of scale,

construction and material dictate layout and appearance. Little consideration is given to quality or durability. The result is that whole sections of the city are now lined with buildings which feel makeshift and shoddy, lacking any sense of permanence. A large percentage of what has been erected in Dublin in the past decade could be taken down again without any architectural loss. These buildings contribute nothing beyond the minimum. Latterly, however, there have been signs of change. As the market for basic apartments with minimal space standards declines, a new market in more 'luxurious' accommodation, aimed at owner-occupiers, is opening up. Architects have suddenly become more attractive to developers. They are seen as adding an extra ingredient to an apartment scheme, rendering what had been merely functional, special. This is not necessarily a very desirable role. Architects might prefer to have a greater say in how sites are used, in ways of engaging the user, in issues of flexibility, of construction, of materiality. That degree of involvement may yet become a reality, but some developers have made a commendable beginning by collaborating with reputable architects on more recent apartment schemes. One such collaboration has resulted in Grafton Architects and Zoe Developments winning a competition for apartments in North King Street, sponsored by Dublin Corporation as part of the HARP Development Plan for the Smithfield area.

In their scheme on North King Street, Grafton Architects have settled on ensuring that some element in each dwelling will have real quality. They *are* making the functional special. Beyond efficiencies of layout and clarity of form, their primary focus has been on the external skin. This has become a sophisticated membrane, capable of mediating between the interior of the apartment and the world outside, between the citizen and the city. The building's principal frontage is on North King Street, to which it presents a sheer five-storey façade. The concrete structure is faced in nine-inch brickwork and the large openings filled with cedarwood shutters and windows. Each apartment has at

least one of these large-scale openings to the street. The moveable timber shutters allow the control of light, air and sound into the interior. Windows may be open while shutters are closed and vice versa. The arrangement of the apartments is straightforward – double frontage, with living running either the full width or from front to back. The spaces feel clean, calm and well ordered. But the great window-opening introduces another order: it negotiates between the scale of the street and the scale of the dwelling. In Louis Kahn's Salk Institute, the timber windows and shutters combine to visually connect the individual research towers to each other and to the great collective space, so that they don't read as isolated openings. In Kahn's Escherick House, each window is accorded a hierarchy of functions – from the introduction of a band of light high up, to the creation of a niche for reading at low level. The window-wall is fundamental to the spatial organisation. Its different subdivisions mark the room it faces, suggesting distances at which an intimate view, a meal, a conversation might occur. People operate in these spaces according to the hierarchy suggested by the windows. In North King Street, the timber windows and screens will assume this role, becoming the anchor and focus of each apartment. The external skin will hold the whole scheme together. This is as true externally at the urban scale as it is internally at the scale of the single dwelling. The street façades bind individual flexibility into a collective unity – the latter has not been sacrificed to the former. The tight staccato rhythm of the openings combines with the deep brick reveals to create a building which feels dense both in its mass and in its programme. Its weight helps it to hold this exposed corner, while its air of intense inhabitation (a colleague described it as 'an urban beehive') celebrates the tight weave of urban life.

The Hall House in Ranelagh is also on a corner site. At a much smaller scale, this project is equally concerned with mediating between the public and the private realm. Its elevations close the site off, drawing brick and stone curtains across it. The house is turned in on itself. Except for a single large opening, it draws most of its light and air from an interior courtyard at first-floor level. Here, the space expands. The L-shaped accommodation and court can be encompassed in a single sweep of the eye. What had seemed closed and weighty suddenly opens out,

becoming light and airy. The concrete structure is held back from the interior glazed wall, its corner left frameless to allow internal space drift out into the court. Ascending to this space, you enter in a different world – an eyrie of light and glass which seems a million miles from the mesh of mews lanes below. The house feels like a cocoon. You are wrapped up into its central chamber and held there, protected from the public realm and yet continuously connected to it through the large window. This window has a curious quality: although it opens the living spaces to clear view, you feel empowered rather than exposed when standing at it. You own the surroundings as much as they own you. You feel curiously invisible, like a child who, eyes shut, believes that no-one can see her. This sensation derives from the powerful sense of place the house creates. Once inside, the outside world is viewed differently. The journey between the street and the living space reconstitutes the relationship between individual and surroundings. In the Eco House competition, this journey involved a complete turning away – the focus was resolutely internal. But the Ranelagh House is more reciprocal in its relationship to context. It withdraws but then re-emerges, like a snail poking its head from a shell.

At Denzille Lane, the relationship between internal and external worlds is differently handled. To the lane, a layer of Reglet glass panels mask an inner layer of glazing, modulating light and view for the apartment behind. The rear apartment, meanwhile, has a fully glazed elevation with sliding timber shutters. Often the best solution to dressing for the Irish climate is to opt for layers that can be donned or shed as the weather shifts. Denzille Lane is clad in this spirit. Its relationship to its context is not fixed. Its relative levels of exposure and enclosure can be altered. Despite the central, organising courtyard, these rich façades feel more like the anchors of the scheme. In Chareau's Maison de Verre, we are constantly drawn to the glass-block skin. Like Kahn's windows, this translucent, glowing membrane masters the spaces it lights. To inhabit Chareau's creation is to oscillate between its two edges. In Denzille Lane, this is equally the case: the building's twin faces define it.

'Assuming that man has a soul,' wrote Kobo Abe, 'it must in all likelihood be housed in the skin.'[2] A lot of recent architecture seems also to have invested its energy and life-force in its skin. For architects as diverse as Jean Nouvel, Peter Zumthor and Herzog and de Meuron, the external cladding has become the focus of intensive experiment and refinement. The thin layer between inside and out controls light, air and atmosphere. At the same time it provides the building with its public face and its private visage. To this extent at least, it *is* the soul of the building. Jacques Herzog has gone so far as to assert that the external wall is now the only built element over which the architect continues to have complete control.[3] And while there is little doubt that Grafton Architects would strongly dispute this claim, would insist on the continuing primacy of space in architecture, it is nonetheless clear that they are according increasing importance to the external envelope of their buildings, and that this envelope is achieving a new autonomy and authority.

Temple Bar Square provides a potent example of this. The project opens up a new urban space in Temple Bar, allowing two large red-brick buildings to face each other across a stone platform. A new building occupies the north side of the square, its façade consisting of an aluminium frame infilled with brick and glass panels. The façade, which owes a debt both to the light industrial idiom of the neighbouring Bad Ass Café and to the long-demolished Retort Building, holds the place together. It provides a poised, rhythmic backdrop to the varied life of the square. The site configuration necessitates a complex organisation of shops and apartments, but from the square little of this intricate manoeuvring is apparent. The calm unity conferred by the framed façade prevails. In his seminal book *Court and Garden*, Michael Dennis describes the Place Vendôme (formerly Place Louis-le-Grand) in Paris:

...the square itself is a stable symmetrical city 'room' hiding, and allowing, the peripheral domestic freedoms beyond. That it conceals the variety around it is its strength, not its weakness, for the requirements of the *res publica* are rarely coincidental with those of the *res privata*, and insistence on integration of the two is as untenable as the complete hegemony of one. The Place Louis-le-Grand exploited the principle of discontinuity to the advantage of both the public and private realms.[4]

The same principle of discontinuity governed the making of Georgian Dublin. The unity of height, proportion, components and materials in a Georgian façade gives it a civic scale, which, in turn licenses luxurious and indulgent decoration in the rooms behind. The Georgian streets and squares enabled the co-existence of public spirit and private freedoms. Looking out from a *piano nobile* window on North Great George's Street, for instance, one immediately senses the correlation between the scale and proportions of the window mullions, and the solids and voids of the façades across the street. The public space rhymes with the private room. At the same time, it does not intrude upon it. *Res publica* and *privata* are in harmony.

In so much of their urban work, Grafton Architects have managed – architecturally – to negotiate a similar pact between city and citizen. The façade becomes the chief intermediary in this exchange. In a way, this is just common sense. It happens in ordinary buildings all the time. But it does run counter to some recent trends in Dublin architecture, where each new creation has tried to assert its unique presence as strongly as possible, often resulting in an uneasy tension between the desire to be a singular object and the willingness to be part of the fabric of the city. This was in large part due to the paucity of opportunities for modern architecture to appear in the city. Every time an opportunity did arise, it was grasped and exploited as fully as possible. But now a different sensibility can be seen emerging, one which sees the value of quietness, which is willing to be more ordinary, to be subsumed into the urban collective. In rural projects like their house at Doolin, Grafton Architects have already been exploring this territory. This is a project which respectfully but firmly adapts a vernacular language of form and material. It is resolutely new, but it doesn't stand out. In their approach to design, Grafton Architects have never relied too heavily on the typological investigations – the search for essential forms which underpinned so much Irish work of the eighties. They have always seemed more interested in qualities of atmosphere and material presence than in formal or organisational precedent. When they borrow from disparate sources to construct the collage elevations with which they have represented many recent projects, it is primarily to suggest experiential and material equivalences: we want it to feel like this, to have the weight and texture of that, the colour and smell of the other. This design tool has become a kind of shorthand which is capable of focussing the energies of a project at an early stage. It can deftly describe the solemn blackness of Trinity's basalt cube, or the heft and poise of the North King Street shutters. It sets out aims to be achieved.

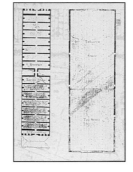

In their recent entry for a limited competition to redevelop part of Dublin's docklands as housing, Grafton Architects envisaged an organisation with the same directness and clarity as the repeated structural bays of an industrial warehouse. Two characteristics of the warehouse in particular – its simple, powerful presence and the calm generosity of its spatial order – offered themselves as useful markers in the search for a new model of urban living. The warehouses which had previously filled the site gave it a consistent grain, like the serried allotments found on eighteenth-century maps of the area. A similar concern for urban grain underlay recent work in Holland, in particular MVRDV's Housing Silo and West 8's master plan for the Borneo-Sporenburg islands in Amsterdam. This Dutch work exhibits a real conceptual freshness and a clear-headed confidence in engaging with the complexities of urban development at a large scale. Dublin certainly needs to be tackled with a similar spirit of energy and innovation. At the moment, the city feels like a gawky teenager. It is growing rapidly, but in different directions, at different rates and in different ways. The capital is inchoate.

Over the next few years, it will have to discover some new, larger, more mature version of itself to carry into the next millennium. If architecture wants to play a substantial part in this transformation then it can no longer afford to confine itself to the insertion of perfectly wrought projects into pockets of the urban fabric. Nor, on the other hand, should it be content with making emptily rhetorical, formalist plans for swathes of the city. Irish architecture needs to become simultaneously more ambitious and more realistic. The city is being shaped by a shifting matrix of commercial, political and social forces which have to be grappled with rather than ignored. Only through a wholehearted engagement with the urban process – often at least as distasteful as it is exhilarating – can architecture hope to exert a meaningful influence on the future form of the urban fabric. More than anything else, what Dublin needs now is a convincing contemporary vernacular. It needs an architecture which accommodates ordinary people doing ordinary things and bestows on these activities some sense of permanence and quality, but an architecture which at the same time helps to reconstitute the public realm. It needs an architecture which is robust and matter-of-fact but is also precisely judged and constructed – an architecture of weight and measure. The docklands competition represented an initial attempt by Grafton Architects to implement such an architecture at a strategic level. Their conceptual clarity, their concern for material presence and the essential humaneness that underpins all their work clearly provide the potent ingredients for a new urban domestic.

Footnotes

[1] Marshall Berman, *All that is Solid Melts into Air – The Experience of Modernity* (Verso Books, New York, 1982), p196
[2] Kobo Abe, *The Woman of the Dunes* (Vintage Books, New York, 1972), p122
[3] Herzog made this comment at a lecture in the Architectural Association, London, in November 1997.
[4] Michael Dennis, *Court and Garden, From the French Hotel to the City of Modern Architecture* (MIT Press, Cambridge, Mass, 1986), p87

Dr Hugh Campbell is a lecturer at the School of Architecture, University College Dublin, where he recently completed his PhD. He has written extensively on urban history and contemporary architecture.

Docklands housing competition
Custom House Docks, Dublin (1998)

The organisation is informed by the site's own history of allotments and warehouses, with a strong north-south grain.

As a strategy, it is a flexible organism, a single structure, which can accommodate both high-rise and low-rise living, with voids forming large public spaces and intimate, secure green spaces. The industrial buildings which previously occupied this site from boundary to boundary had an urban scale within the repetitive structure.

The intention of the proposed singular structure was, similarly, to build the site rather than place buildings on the site.

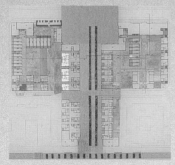

10

Rational
Pleasures

INTERVIEW BY RAYMUND RYAN

Raymund Ryan – Let's begin at the beginning. You are both from rural towns and I know you take the fabric of such towns very seriously indeed. How has childhood or adolescence in Lisdoonvarna, Tullamore and other Irish towns influenced your subsequent careers?

Yvonne Farrell – One good thing about coming from towns in rural Ireland is that you don't have an unduly romantic view of either the city or the countryside. Tullamore was burned down and then rebuilt as a planned town. So my childhood memory is of streets and squares, as well as being able to leave the back of the house and run into the countryside. You had the town very strong as a form, and you had landscape. We are very conscious that we come from that kind of Irish urban tradition.

Shelley McNamara – Yvonne's point is a very good one about not having that separation between urban and rural. In recent projects in the countryside, we have gone back to places and buildings we've known over long periods of time, and found inspiration, in particular, in farm and agricultural buildings, in their simplicity and honesty in terms of construction.

What stimulated each of you to study architecture?

S – Part of the reason I was interested in architecture is that I came from a building background. But that didn't guarantee that it would necessarily work out for me.

Y – When we were students, I used to visit Shelley's home, and there was always that sense that their house was about making. It *was* a construction company, a very attractive environment to observe. I think my own interest in architecture stemmed from two things – a pleasure in making things and a curiosity, in some way, about people.

The UCD School of Architecture had come through a period of turmoil in the early seventies. Which teachers or events influenced you?

S – Going through the School of Architecture then was a very intense experience. As in most years, there was a group of us who influenced and inspired each other. That was very formative. Plus the teaching that we had. Ivor Smith had just been appointed Head of the School, and he was a very driven and focused educationalist.

Y – The 'Flying Circus' [Chris Cross, Fenella Dixon, Jeremy Dixon, Mike Gold and Ed Jones] came in weekly from London and made such an impact on the school. They had such clarity. They were like a rock band – just by their energy they raised the whole tone of the school. They were very enthusiastic teachers, and their enthusiasm was contagious.

S – Their generosity was combined with intelligence and an articulate expression of architecture. John Miller and Alan Colquhoun also came as visiting critics.

At UCD in the late seventies you were all lumped together as the Corb Squad. Why was Le Corbusier a bigger influence than, say, Mies or Aalto?

Y – The sculptural quality. His structural rigour. The form and the plasticity of it was so attractive. He had a fantastic range of opportunities in his work. Each project was taken afresh. Studying Corb's work was really a kind of apprenticeship. I interpreted Mies as being more limited. Mies was more about closing and refining, whereas Corb was more open.

S – And I suppose we reacted against the organic component in Aalto's work. It seemed too loose, although I've now changed that assessment. We took on the work of Corb and learned about architecture through that work. In a way, it's a reflection on the educational process at the time, which wasn't as broad-ranging and eclectic as it is now.

Y – Years later, when we did the two mews houses in Clyde Lane, we had obviously studied La Roche Jeanneret, the twin houses for a businessman and an artist. For me, La Roche Jeanneret is one of the most beautiful of Corb's buildings. It is on the cusp of change from a kind of Arts and Crafts into a more rigorous, intellectual thrust.

Vincent Scully highlights Le Corbusier's ability to make extraordinary single buildings and his urban proposals which would have destroyed central Paris. How do you integrate the inheritance of Modernity with the broader inheritance of our cities?

S – The differentiation between Le Corbusier's ability to make extraordinary single buildings and his urbanistic proposals is, I think, valid. But there's an urban component in his way of thinking which imbues his buildings with another sensibility, which I think is critical to the success of the buildings.

Y – The social content of Corb's work – the relationship of the individual with the collective – really caught our imagination. His Unité apartment building is a vertical village.

S – And it is very exciting to meet children on bicycles in the lifts going up to terraces on the roof. We thought a lot about that when we were doing the Docklands competition: how do you make apartment buildings that can support that kind of life? Yes, as masterplans go, there is an issue there. But in terms of Le Corbusier's individual buildings, I think that the radical urban component made them much more poignant

Y – You know that terrific image of the Unité, of the timber inset sliding into the concrete mould of the unit? In our project for the Eco House competition, there are softer elements inserted into the integrated crust of services and materials that hold it together.

S – Modernism in the city is no longer about a particular style; it is more about trying to pick up on the character of a place. It is thinking about modernism in terms not of language, but of resonance. That is something we tried to do in North King Street – to make a modern building that has a sense of warehouse. It is a very interesting development within modernity in general, that sometimes it can take a more modest role.

There is a sense of that in the Kinvara house, of knitting the house into its context.

S – That is also true of Doolin and Westport. It is almost as if they haven't been designed by architects. There's a kind of

accumulation of vernacular elements put together in a certain kind of way. It is to do with continuity and tradition. For us, the lesson of those projects was about getting to the essence of very simple, direct buildings.

Y – At Temple Bar Square, we were trying, at one level, to 'play' with surface and context in an informal way. But another way of reading the Temple Bar Square façade is as a very tight skin, not unlike the surfaces of Georgian squares, which are really very strict – they are sheer walls.

S – The industrial language was also relevant because of the nature of Temple Bar itself and because of the adjacent Bad Ass

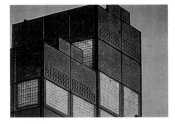

Café. We were trying to use steel and brick in a very tough way, like the 1950s Retort Building, which we looked at a lot. And now it is gone – one of Dublin's biggest architectural losses!

Y – I think our work is increasingly about such layers, layers of meaning and layers of surface. Many of the school projects are about extending an existing complex or adding a new element. We like to interpret the old and new – not just as the built old and new, but also as a geological old and new. For example, with the Castleblayney project, we're trying to engage with the landscape, and to absorb the landscape into the form of the building.

Kenneth Frampton's concept of Critical Regionalism might well be applied to your work. How do you see your projects enhancing place? In what ways do you believe your work is critical?

Y – Well, the physical context of our buildings is really important. We don't have an in-house style; we don't aspire to being fashionable. Each project begins by trying to understand space and function, and by getting to know the place physically. Architecture is also part of our culture and heritage, and we have a responsibility to extend that legacy.

S – We look at buildings in the area. In Celbridge, we visited the big houses and institutional buildings in the area and studied their whole approach to landscaping. You have to get a sense of how buildings in the locale connect with the ground.

In what way do we believe our work is critical? Maybe it is to do with the stage you are at within a particular strain of work. Through work, our agenda or direction has definitely become more focused. Probably the most critical thing is to get the character of a building right – to work from the character back to the language as opposed to working from the language to the character.

With the project in Trinity, a lot of things came together. It is such a wonderful campus, but the geometry and edges of the site were very complicated. We started with models and three-dimensional drawings. It was a volumetric problem, actually, how to sit a building in this amazing place.

Y – When we went to the site, there were two mature lime trees which are magnificent creatures. We wanted to contribute to the organic nature of the site. So we read it as the cube being the abstract and then the landscape washing up to the edge of the site as the organic.

When you talk about projects, you often refer to atmosphere and to character.

Y – In the schools projects, we try to make a strong sense of place. The courtyard in the Oughterard school is a reinterpretation of the Irish cloister tradition, of the monastery in the landscape. The school in Celbridge is arrang-
ed around a large garden space, and is related more to the walled gardens and refined landscaping of nearby demesnes. So even though Celbridge is a rapidly expanding town, there will always be this place held as an ideal.

S – It is about dealing with the basic elements of building in order to make architecture. In Trinity, it was a combination of curtain walls and traditional ways of using stone cladding – trying to think of the stone cube as a big solid block. Later, it is able to transfer into something like the house in Ranelagh. Denzille Lane is a development of Temple Bar Square which is about a thinner skin. It is trying to deal with steel and glass, taking light deep into the building, and the density of the section.

The value of density is that you create more plastic complexity but also encourage people to interact.

Y – We value density as a positive thing. We also value structure and complexity. The plastic nature of how work is done allows us to respond to peculiarity, and that can add to atmosphere.

In our school projects, we're acutely aware that we are building for the students and teachers. We try to find some specific quality in each project, to give each school a strong sense of place. The circulation areas are where social interaction happens. So we put energy into making these spaces special – the ideal courtyard at Celbridge, the undulating corridors at Castleblayney.

Is it possible to include the unforeseeable future uses of a building in the design process? Is this where typology is of particular value to your work?

S – I think typology is a trap in many ways because it is a sort of shorthand, which sometimes means that you miss the essential.

Y – I think what is liberating about a typology is that you have at your disposal, because of experience, a wide range of organisations and spaces that can be useful in particular situations.

S – In the Docklands and North King Street, because of those locations, the typology is warehouse construction. Ideally, a lot of buildings that were demolished wouldn't have been, and people could just live in fantastic big open spaces. How do you make a large urban building which is versatile and intimate? That was our interest in the Docklands competition. Recently we've found it more important to get under the surface of an issue, to see it from another point of view. So maybe we're taking typologies for granted. Or else maybe we're shedding them.

Y – I think they are resources that we've inherited, and now we either use them or we distort them. For us, the critical issue is the people who are going to use the building. That's why we make models – we're trying to communicate. The more actively clients work with us, the more they understand what's happening. It is not like we make a sealed object and that's it.

S – In today's city, public space needs to be strong to survive the continuous intensity of use. Buildings really have to be very robust. It is a real challenge to make a building that can survive the unforeseeable.

I was thinking of Rossi's model of the Basilica in Vicenza which has grown and shrunk over the centuries to accommodate things that couldn't have been imagined when it was first built.

S – It is the idea of universal space.

Y – I don't think we see things as being totally finite. Some of the projects are formally complete and are difficult to add to. Others are more open-ended, especially the schools, I suppose, because schools tend to grow if they're successful. Another issue touching upon that is one of maintenance, or how a building looks long after it is built.

It raises the issue of weathering in Ireland. It doesn't have to be a negative thing.

S – That's true about weathering. As you get more mature, you can take it on more seriously. To do the most with the minimum, and to take on issues of robustness and structure and time. It is quite shocking that Aalto's buildings are so *amazing* through time. They are just incredible the way they have weathered. So beautiful!

I have long admired your scheme for the Cliffs of Moher, the way it inhabits the ground and proposes its collage of materials. Can you explain this fascination with the skin of buildings?

S – The Cliffs of Moher project was a turning point in our work because that was the first time we thought of a building as a piece of landscape.

It was also the first time you used collage, wasn't it?

S – Yes. The medium is a shorthand for dealing with materials parallel to dealing with organisation, for making the projects more about character and texture.

Y – The presentation panels for the competition became tactile in themselves, rather than being a series of line drawings. They became our study. The skin of the building came from those fantastic stone walls that are there. The project was conceived as a ruin with great slabs of Liscannor slate.

Many of the projects – the houses in Ranelagh and Kinvara, for example – are carefully balanced compositions. How useful a criterion is composition?

Y – I don't think it is a lightweight appliqué of an idea. I feel that composition is part of our remit or responsibility as architects. For composers of music, the actual form and shape and skin, if you like, of a piece is important. Listening to contemporary music, sometimes the discord is hard to follow if you enjoy Baroque pieces…

The music analogy is a very nice one. If you took composition out of music, music as we know it wouldn't exist.

Y – Composition is natural to design. It is the painterly aspect of form – is it not? – to get the three-dimensionality and the materials working.

S – In this respect, the Hall House is not an abstract composition brought to the site. It is responding to a very tall brick gable on the one side, and a terrace of two-storey houses on the other. And the materials came out of the immediate context. Compositionally, it is about changing scale.

There is a point when volumetric composition is almost like a different discipline to elevational composition, which is about rhythm and repetition. With housing, it is about repetition; you're trying to *hold* surface and get beyond the very particular scale of the rooms behind it. It has to have a civic quality, this wall which is neutral on the one hand but inhabited on the other. I suppose that maybe composition and abstraction are very directly connected.

Y – It is interesting that the 'machine' of the individual has expression, but within a disciplined or restricted palate. Going back to issues of character – in the North King Street project, each individual person can affect the composition of the building by the language of the shutters. The material which is moveable – the timber – allows for individuality. And the brick, then, is the solid piece that doesn't change.

I think the direction of the work is towards abstraction, that there is a growing interest in abstracting even the most mundane, functional requirements.

We haven't talked about how the office functions. Do you perform identical roles? What is the input of your employees and two associates?

S – The history of the office is important in terms of the way we function. We started out as a co-operative practice. In some ways, we've inherited that attitude to work. Yes, we direct it and we hold it, but we do really try to make a culture within which people can contribute. That is of value to us and hopefully of value to them. A number of people have made huge contributions, particularly Philippe [O'Sullivan] and Ger [Carty], who have been with us for some time and are now associates in the practice. They are part of our core team and are contributing to the development and direction of the practice.

Y – Another key issue is that teaching is one aspect of our lives, and making is the other, and they're not in completely separate compartments. I think they overlap.

S – I think the most civilised thing about our office is that there is a ritual every day, at coffee, of discussing work, whether it is a problem that somebody has, or a success.

Y – That's the important thing about models. The model becomes, if you like, office property, and there are discussions about it. There's a lot of responding. And there's a lot of responding on site. Hopefully, the relationships beyond the office, particularly with the clients and the builders, inform the work in a certain kind of way.

Which buildings have impressed you recently? What are your own aspirations for future architectural projects?

S – Siza's church at Marco de Canaveses I found very moving. There is an innocence about his work, combined with an amazing sophistication. He transforms Modernism into something completely Portuguese. The last time I felt as strongly about a contemporary building was probably Corb's Assembly Building at Chandigarh. It was so shockingly beautiful!

Y – Two buildings spring to mind. The first is Ronchamp, which is tiny and intimate, yet an incredible vessel. And that great door which opens out in celebration to the landscape! The other is a public laundry in Porto, with no elevation. You ramp down into a cave-like washing area with a rooflight which becomes a bench in the plaza overhead. So it is total integration and total non-ego.

So are they the kind of impressions you would like your own work to make?

Y – Hmmm, that would be wonderful, to enable people react to a building, that they remember it as something pleasurable. When you deal with buildings very rationally – to get qualities of light or to get qualities of place – you really have to fight for those kind of things. I suppose that skill comes with experience. It would be lovely to attain it sometimes. Maybe every project has a little place that is getting more and more successful.

S – If I were to say what my own aspirations are for future architectural projects, it is that search really to try and hit something emotional, to hit the emotional component of work as well as the practical. I think it is very, very hard to do.

Raymund Ryan is an architectural graduate of UCD and Yale University. He is a contributing editor to *Blueprint*, and has contributed to journals and catalogues worldwide.

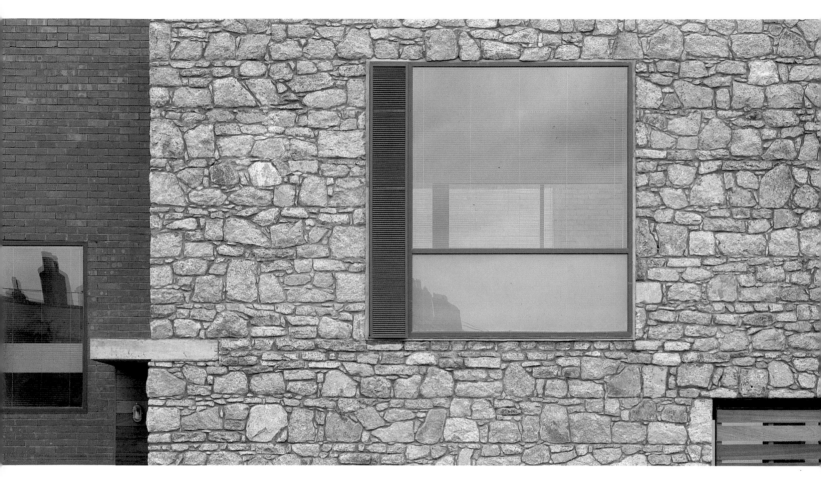

Hall House
Ranelagh, Dublin 6 (1999)

Temple Bar Square
Dublin 2 (1992-96)
(Group 91 / Grafton Architects)

Temple Bar Square is the junction of
one of the main north-south pedestrian
routes, linking Temple Bar with the rest
of the city. The development comprises
a public space, five commercial units of
varying sizes, and nine residential units.

The architecture is influenced by the
industrial character of many buildings
in the area, but is more particularly
influenced by the Gas Retort Building
formerly in Dublin's docklands.
This building had a monumental
industrial character, and consisted of a
steel grid with brick and glass-block
infill panels.

below
– location map
– ground-floor plan

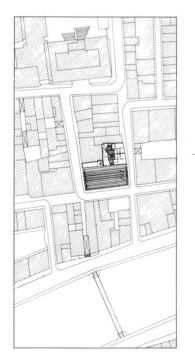

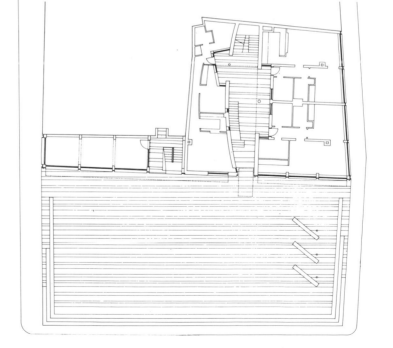

The metal framework is common to the three elements of the façade, i.e. the 12ft-deep glass and steel building clipped onto the existing Bad Ass Café gable, the central 'anchor' element with a large steel gateway to the apartments, and the corner brick block which turns onto Fownes Street. The language of the elevation is the working of a taut skin of metal and brick. The skin has two layers; only two special corner windows at first-floor level are integrated into the outer layer. Engineering brick was used because of its sheen and hardness, and its likeness to metal. The tiny retail units in the Bad Ass façade have the character of market stalls. The private courtyard to the apartments is tall and narrow, with a dramatic view to the square.

– eastern end elevation and section

opposite
– looking down Fownes Street towards the river
– views of the interior courtyard
– section showing access to apartments

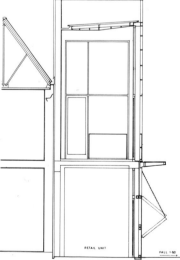

Mind – matter of cool passion

ELIZABETH HATZ

Mouth-blown glass transmits nearly 30% more light into a room than industrial glass. It is wafer thin, and its hundreds of irregularities, minute air bubbles, cysts and impurities act as prisms in a crystal chandelier, breaking and amplifying the light rays that move as abstract patterns on adjacent walls like incessantly changing pictures. Mouth-blown glass blurs and distorts the view at some distance, creating from within and without a thin, crinkled membrane – a subtle, yet materially manifest separation of the two worlds. It would be strange to believe that people who used this glass were totally unaware of or insensitive to those diverse practical and poetic conditions. It would be equally strange to think ourselves incapable of discerning such qualities in materials at hand now.

When Grafton Architects, for the Mechanical Engineering building at Trinity College, travel to the continent in search of the cladding for their enigmatic black cube, this kind of discerning sensitivity is at work. The very concentration is right here. The basalt isn't black; it acts black. The box isn't a cube; it acts cubical. No material nostalgia, but utter, daring inventiveness in search of the proper tone, a tone to mislead premature conceptions of what this building is, what all its parts are, what its matter is. At a distance, the solidity of the bold, blackish cube sits like a corner stone in the complicated geometry of this side of the campus, giving to it the anchoring mass proper for an institution. But this is achieved not through size, for it is, in reality, quite small, but through consistency of form. Yet, the relative softness of the black basalt cladding, and the way this form at certain angles becomes reflective, actually adds to its own partial dissolution, or at least to a more ambiguous, evasive appearance. Its solidity thus becomes a mind matter, since what the material refuses to affirm still grows stronger as an abstraction restoring its presence in the mind. So, what is stated with form and massing – black cube, granite base – is modified and made uncertain by the material-making, but also by a geometri-

cal device. The dressed cube hovers on glass over the sliding granite base. The horizontality and spiralling movement up to the terrace is weaving the building into its setting, as part of the shared campus ground. This base, however, is anything but solid: horizontal slots make it all see-through, between terrace, workshop and street pavement. The cube that seemed dominant contains the smaller rooms, while in the flatter base, you discover the big, dynamic workspace with its sexy columns. This way, the relatively small building manages to set up a certain institutional authority in its overall shape and setting, while a closer acquaintance invites surprising views into its own intimacy and immediate situation. I believe this is one of the characteristics that reoccur in the work of Grafton Architects: the elegantly simple geometry of composition unravels, at closer encounter, an ambiguity and emotional charge that makes the work come alive as spatial opportunity for human affairs, rather than retracting to the harmless, object-centred category where so much contemporary architecture ends up.

The choice and handling of materials is careful, precise, but also surprising, elusive, or evocative, making you sense the building rather than reading it as a sign where the materials enter as representations of given ideas. Grafton architecture is not coded message or image; it is much more dangerously entering action and emotion. Hence, the almost-black almost-cube is loosely clad in the soft, oblique, elusive basalt, like a veil, forcing you to reconstitute the cube in your mind. Despite the obvious minimalist language, this architecture has more associations with, for instance, A & P Smithson and their way of fusing what the building does and what it is, as a robust conglomerate of conditions from within.

All this strikes me as the witful, obstinate, and utterly poetic stream that seems to flow through some of the best contemporary Irish architecture. But this built wit, this way of making you

22

lose the meaning just as you thought you had found it, this way of forcing you to question your senses is also engaging all your senses.

The art of Grafton Architects is made through building: into the sum of the characteristics enter the profound bodily condition. So, the refined competition scheme for the Ecological Pavilion is entirely within the theme. Be it a school, a campus building, or a townhouse, the fabric itself seems the crucial element for constituting the core, the abstract quality of the intricate geometric play in the building, for the benefit of the inhabitation of it.

In several projects, this seems to deal with a three-dimensional rotation, a spiralling route. A variation of this is at work in the Hall House. As a counterweight to the domesticity of the task and setting, here the geometric composition is exposed emblematically in the exterior. It shows a geometry of apparent added flatnesses creating apparent frontalities, yet stepping and sliding the corner of the block to create minute, half-domesticated zones at the perimeter. The simplicity of the stark exterior that settles the corner of the site tremendously, while charging it with both monumentality and intimacy, thus mediating the two scales of the streets, is again of defeating simplicity when you come to the interior landscape of the house.

How can tightness create spatial abundance? How can discipline of geometry and structure give intimacy and sensuous diversity? The space itself within the Hall House is unfolding like a complex organism, while surfaces act as neat and strict backdrops. The sophistication of this spatial dance is even hard to convey through photography. The fact is that the Hall House, through its tight geometry of pushing and pulling the volumes to encompass also all these hard-to-define secondary spaces that turn ordinary domesticity into a *cittá picolla* – the perilous place where high and low, formal, private and unpredictable confront – becomes a microcosmos, a delicately shifting prism of light and time. Interiors fuse into terraces, borrowing naturally adjacent walls with neon signs, so the house both invites and eats itself into the existing city fabric. This meandering geometry also acts as an upheaval of the vertical hierarchical division of private and common spaces. After a while in this house, with its vistas, nooks and crannies, I realise that it is like a garden, a garden reflecting, in miniature, a landscape. The strictness of detail is an absolute necessity, as is the sense of control and measure. The presence of this control is passion, but also reverence for the matter that this measure enhances. The slick surface of the brick, responding to the ceramic quality of the neighbouring bar, reflects the light and seems to expand that surface as if the little corner was larger, thus ending the block with some solemnity in its sparse fenestration.

What is apparent in the Trinity building, the Hall House, and several other projects is the refusal to rely on features. The architects' own reference in the interview to an anonymous Portuguese laundry without elevation – 'total integration and total non-ego' – as well as the reference to the 'emotional component' in architecture, well describe the delicate and profound territory of the Grafton group, making, I believe, one very long-lasting quality of their work.

As a rather large conglomerate of buildings, the Celbridge Community School sits very elegantly in the landscape. This is due to a careful and very consistent sense of massing, pressing the volumes towards the ground like huge slopes, and at the same time, creating a type of internal topography where the different parts become incidents and identities. This adds up to give a certain drama to the large scale, as in surrounding vistas, while giving a kind of narrative intimacy to the internal spaces, like a path of separate stories strung like beads. Again, a spiralling string. Despite clear association to architects like Aalto and Siza, this work therefore remains stubbornly and seductively Irish in all its modernity – self-reliant and controlled. While there is absolute clarity in respect of adjacency of functions and structural consistency, there is a way of interconnecting, shaping, detailing and massing the elements which starts to create subtle conversations with the site. Overlappings, alternative routes and views are weaving into the very body and structure of the work a poetic, irrational dimension.

Elizabeth Hatz is professor of architecture at KTH School of Architecture in Stockholm, and runs her own private practice. Published in *Arkitektur* and *Mama Magazine* in Sweden.

Screening room for
Clarence Pictures
Denzille Lane, Dublin 2 (1996-99)

The site is a long, narrow mews slot to the rear of 13 Merrion Square. The programme is to provide a purpose-built screening room, associated office and reception facilities and two apartments.

The scheme is organised by an external cascading stairs which cuts a slot from the ground-floor forecourt to the raised second-floor courtyard, and allows light to be drawn into the depth of the long, narrow plan. The office and apartments open off the raised courtyard.

The elevation to the lane is developed as an abstract screen of clear and sand-blasted glass, glass planking and stainless steel framing. The screen provides privacy, ventilation and select views. The elevation towards the main house, by contrast, is clad in cedar boarding framed in stainless steel.

– model
– site section and plan
  1 – forecourt
  2 – video-editing
  3 – courtyard
  4 – duplex apartment
  5 – garden
  6 – No.13 Merrion Square
     with garden room extension
– garden elevation
– screening room
– reception area / bar

opposite
– forecourt
– cascading staircase
– elevation to Denzille Lane

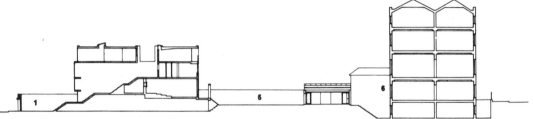

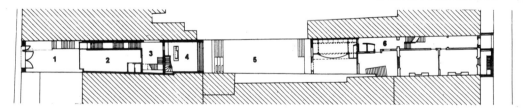

Office Building
Little Strand Street, Dublin 7 (1997-98)

This three-storey office building is located on a small street off Capel Street. The principal elevation has a northerly aspect, and has graduated levels of transparency from glass-block to clear glass. The materials and scale relate to an adjacent stone warehouse. Cedar wood openable ventilators are distributed through the glass and glass-block walls, which are unified by a single stainless steel support frame.

– elevation to Little Strand Street
– site plan
– elevation detail

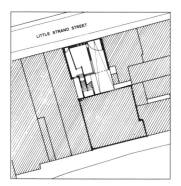

North King Street apartments
Smithfield, Dublin 7 (1997-99)
(for Zoe Developments and
Dublin Corporation)

This scheme for 66 apartments aims to
produce a building which has a calm
modesty. The building sits 'solid' on the
ground, and has a sense of weight and
permanence. Design features are
deliberately avoided in an attempt to
regain the quiet monumental presence
of adjacent warehouse buildings.
This scheme seeks to interpret this
language using a rational load-bearing
structure, setting up a loose rhythm of
openings across the façade – a non-
stylistic expression, a type of neutrality
which can accommodate both sleeping
and living spaces. There is a vertical
emphasis to the elevation – traditional
to Dublin street architecture.

A series of large doorways provides
access from the street to the
apartments. Common gateways and
arches provide access to the protected
courtyard. The street wall is 53cm thick,
and is constructed of brick and timber
with large sliding shutters, which offer
security, privacy, environmental and
acoustic protection from the busy
streets. The courtyard walls, by
contrast, are constructed of brick, steel
and glass.

– site plan (ground floor)
– cross-section
– upper floor plan

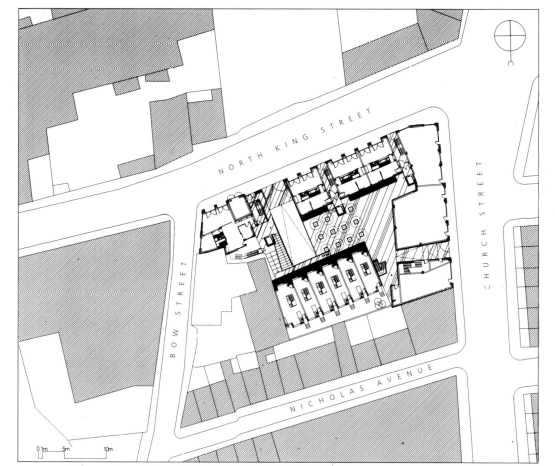

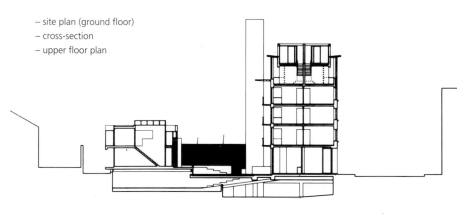

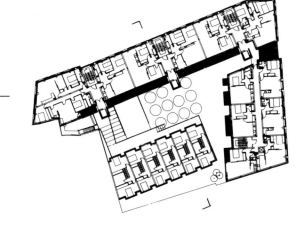

North King Street
– model showing view from Church
  Street / North King Street corner
– concept sketch of courtyard
– elevation study (North King Street)
– North King Street elevation

opposite
– views of the building under
  construction

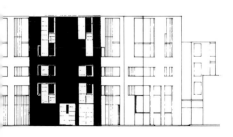

Dept of Mechanical and Manufacturing Engineering
Trinity College, Dublin 2 (1994-96)

This project consists of a 1,100m² extension to the 19th-century Parson's Building. While the main geometry of the campus is orthogonal, the granite Parson's Building sat alone, elevated, at an angle to its surroundings.

A heavy stone base, clad in robust Wicklow granite, houses the bulk of the workshop and engineering laboratories. The roof of this space forms a podium and forecourt to the Parson's Building. Rooflights in this podium light the workshops below.

Above the podium, a raised 'cube' houses the Fluids and Acoustic Engineering Laboratory. The cube is aligned to the formal geometry of the campus. It is clad in a dark, reflective basalt lava.

– concept sketch
– perspectives and section
– study model
– site model
– site plan (new building highlighted)

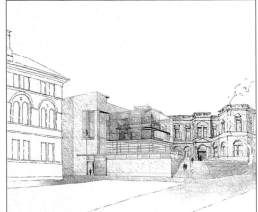
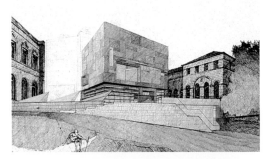
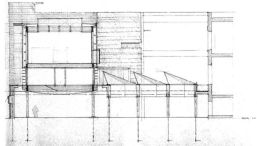

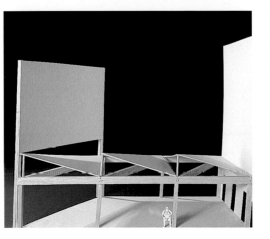
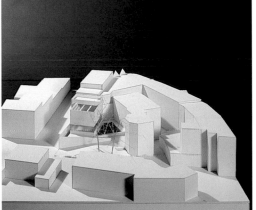

A taller element, the 'book-end', is finished in a highly polished pigmented plaster. This houses the seminar rooms, and its tall sliding metal door and lifting beam allow for deliveries to the laboratories.

Two existing mature lime trees are retained, forming an essential part of the landscape character of the project. The raised cube, the Parson's Building and the lime trees now form part of a new enclosure. The three elements – the new, the old and the organic – make a new place within the walls of the university.

opposite
– view of building from playing fields
– elevation study
– section through laboratories
– ground-floor plan

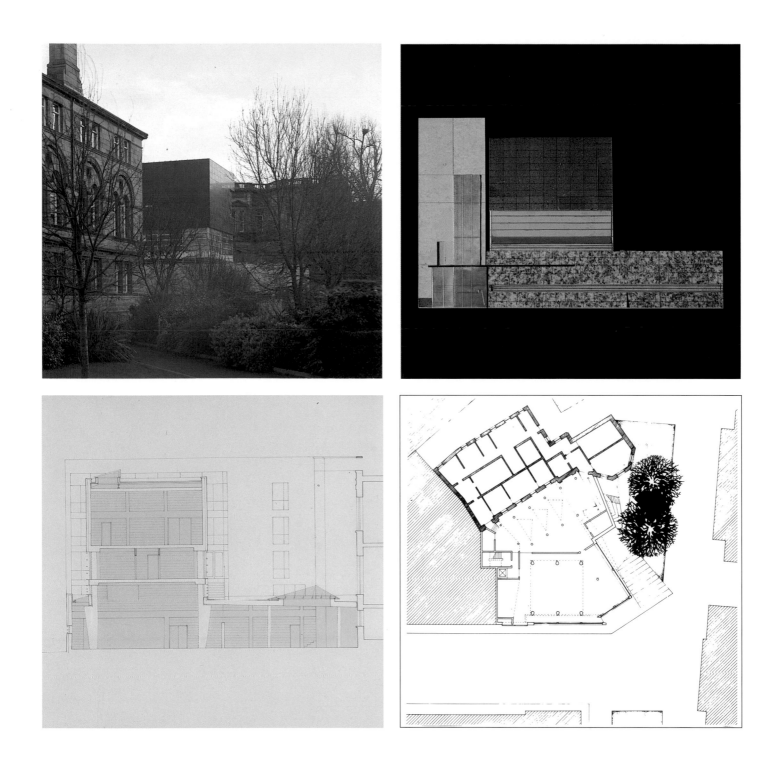

Dept of Mechanical and
Manufacturing Engineering
– the new building in context
– raised podium with rooflights to
  workshops below
– office interior
– part-section

opposite
– ground-floor workshops, with large
  columns supporting 'cube' above

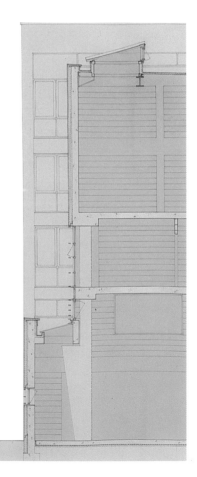

Celbridge Community School
Co Kildare (1996-99)
(for the Dept of Education and Science)

The school for 700 pupils is arranged around a large garden space. A concrete 'ribbon' canopy weaves its way around two sides of the garden.

The scheme is influenced by the walled gardens and the refined landscaping of nearby demesnes. Never rising more than two floors, the building hugs the land. There is a deliberate 'flattening' of the building, with long shallow roofs creating a sense of the building connecting with the ground, and at times merging with it, when viewed from certain vantage points. This sense of 'flattening' is reinforced by the landscaping on the eastern and southern edges, with mounds of earth forming shallow slopes to form enclosure and intimacy.

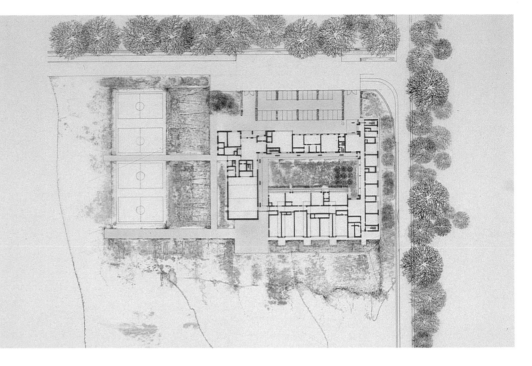

The boundaries of the site to the north and west are strongly defined by a stone wall and by a band of beautiful, mature deciduous trees. The entrance space, at right angles to the road, is formed by the long, low elevation of the building, addressing this strong band of trees. Beech hedges establish the car park and pedestrian entrance spaces.

– model of school
– interior view
– sections
– courtyard view to south

opposite
– site plan
– main entrance and west elevation

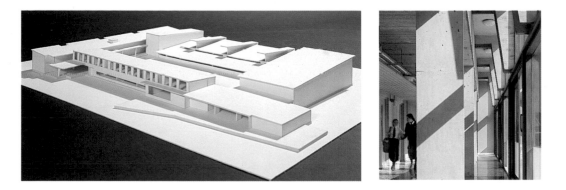

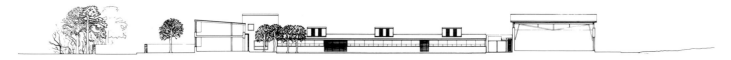

Our Lady's Secondary School
Castleblaney, Co Monaghan (1995-99)

This three-storey extension, comprising new classrooms and specialist teaching areas, is built on the sloping hills at the edge of the existing school precinct. This extension places the new front door of the school close to the town.

The plan of the building, with its parallel bands of rooms on either side of a wide corridor, is cranked to follow the contours of the hillside. The ground-floor corridor ramps gently, and connects with the existing school. Light-scoops direct natural light to the lower corridor, and the upper corridor is lit by a continuous east-facing clerestory window. This 30m-long space was conceived of as a 'nave', with its roof sloping parallel with the contours. The scale of this space is expressed in the

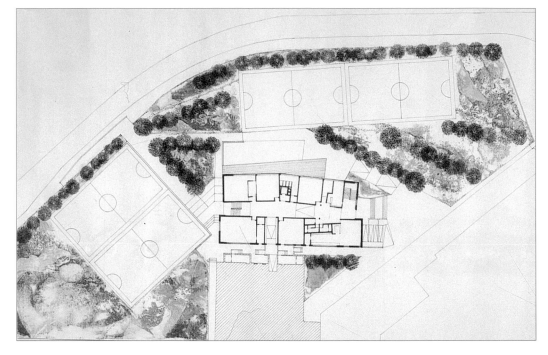

end elevations, where the nave comes
to the edge and forms large doorways
into the school.

Earth mounds, retaining walls and
ramps form and contain the arrival
space, the playing courts and the
landscape adjacent to the building.

– model
– interior views
– cross-section through classrooms and
  corridor with light-scoop
– north entrance
– light-scoop under construction
– detail of main façade

opposite
– site plan
– the main façade of the school

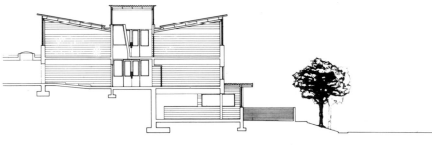

Coláiste Eoin / Coláiste Íosagáin
Stillorgan, Co Dublin (1997-99)

This project is for the extension of two established schools which share the same site. The project has two defined formal elements – a large gymnasium and a four-storey classroom block – which are placed close to a wooded area at the northern edge of the site. Landscaping and other new-built elements connect them to one another and to existing single-storey buildings.

The gymnasium forms a new edge to existing playing courts. It is profiled to lean towards the front, forming a canopy for shelter while eliminating glare from the sun. Workshops and labs are placed at the base of the classroom block. The form is fractured at the upper levels to make a south-facing, raised courtyard which forms an 'eye' towards the Dublin mountains.

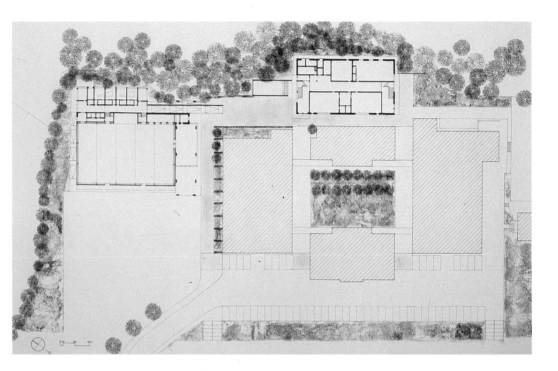

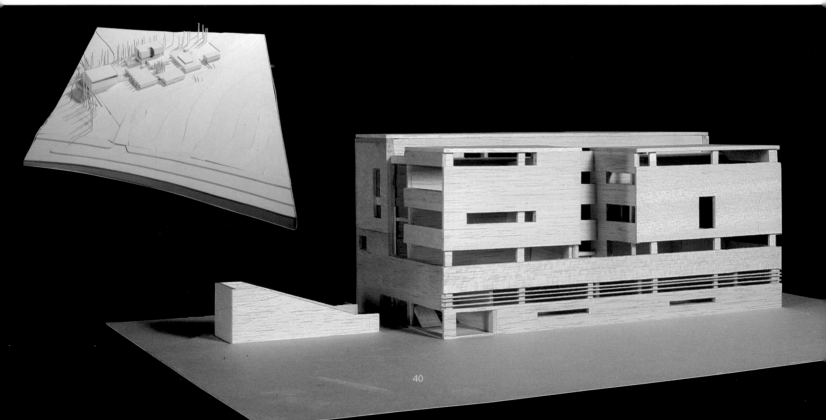

Civic Centre
Dunshaughlin, Co Meath (1997-99)

The intention of this project is to make a modern public building which will have an accessible, welcoming, civic character; a building which will improve with the patina of time, has an integrated approach to services and flexibility, and minimises the need for mechanical heating and cooling.

The skeleton of the building is in-situ concrete, exposed throughout, with timber and glass infill screens.
All service routes are integrated into accessible floor and wall ducts, and the building will be 95% self-sufficient in terms of heating and cooling.

The building consists of a number of key elements:
– the cantilevered entrance canopy (made of concrete, with glass infill)
– the main public information hall (designed as a 'nave', which acts as a heat collector and distributor, and containing a double-wall which houses the services of the building)
– the inner information hall (with reflected natural light, and sound-absorbant study alcoves)
– the council chamber (which also has a double-wall: an outer wall of white and clear glass, an inner wall of timber screens and sliders)
– the urban space and car park (with landscaping and lighting to suit both pedestrian and vehicular use)

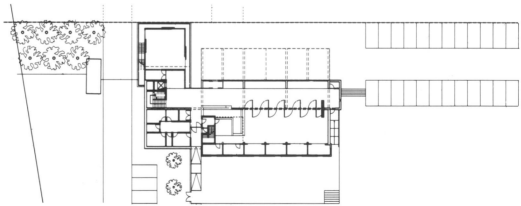

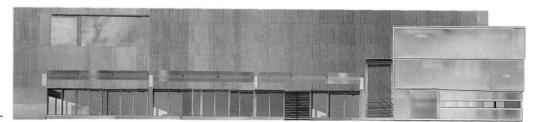

Motorway Bridge
Killarney Road, Bray, Co Wicklow
(1994-95) (with Roughan O'Donovan)

This bridge crosses the main Dublin-Wexford road in an important picturesque location in Co Wicklow.

The brief was to design a new bridge over a live dual-carriageway, and so the form of deck construction was limited to pre-cast concrete beams. In order to overcome the flat and static nature of this type of deck, the in-situ concrete elements – central columns and diaphragm beam, abutments and fascia – were used to give some expression to the bridge. The fascia is curved to express the span, and the abutments are designed as anchors into the earth.

opposite

Motorway Bridge
Balbriggan, Co Dublin (1995-98)
(with Roughan O'Donovan)

This bridge crosses the main Dublin to Belfast motorway. It sits in the flat landscape of north Co Dublin.

It is a tapered, in-situ concrete bridge, springing from a central, flat, oval-shaped pier. The depth of the deck tapers to the edges, and the abutments rise out of the ground to receive the deck. The joint between deck and abutment is accentuated to give a sense of lightness to the bridge ends. The proportion and shape of the central pier is designed to have a sense of mass and weight, in contrast with the lighter deck.

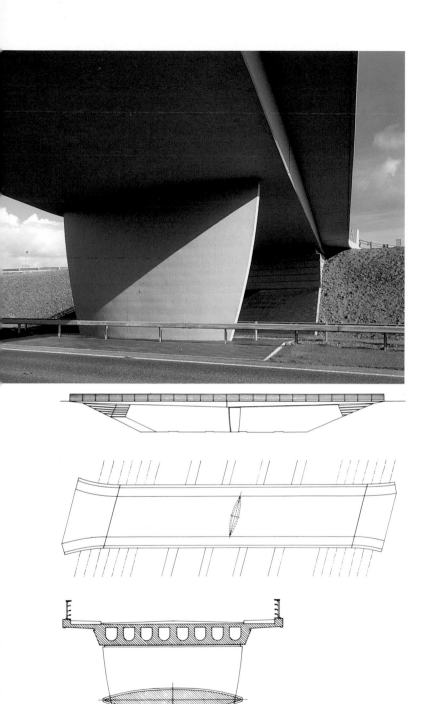

Gray and O'Connell House
Doolin, Co Clare (1993-95)

This is a house for a batik artist, a jeweller and their two children. It is located on the west coast of Ireland, with a distant view of the Atlantic Ocean and the Cliffs of Moher.

The planning requirement was for a 'strictly' traditional elevation to the main road. The reference point was the middle-sized farmhouse, common in this area, which is a long, thin house, one room deep, with simple, plain surface treatment to the external wall.

The site is extremely exposed to south-west winds. This long house forms one wall of an enclosed courtyard which faces south. The walls of the courtyard are free-standing 'wind screens', with openings to set up and intensify the relationship with the sea, the cliffs and the surrounding landscape.

The plan is quite free and open, with a glazed, double-height space forming the heart of the house.

above
– north elevation
below
– south-facing courtyard
– ground-floor plan

Mara House
Kinvara, Co Galway (1995-98)

This scheme occupies an existing walled site overlooking Kinvara pier, Dunguaire Castle, and Galway Bay. The existing quayside wall consists of small-scale houses, a large stone grainstore, and remnants of stone boundary walls.

The main house and two smaller holiday houses sit within the existing walls, forming a forecourt between the houses and the public quayside.

The language of the new walls and shutters stems from vernacular farm buildings, offering layers of protection from the sea winds, security when not in use in the winter, and privacy from the active quay in high season.

above
– view from Kinvara quayside
below
– detail of new stone wall and shutters
– site plan

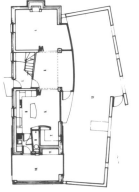

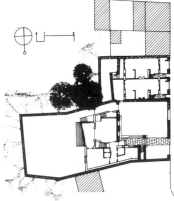

Gill House
Westport, Co Mayo (1995-98)

This site overlooks the dramatic Clew Bay, and is subject to some of the strongest winds on the western seafront. The house sits on a sloping site, and consists of three elements, each at different levels, which 'cluster' to form a protected entrance courtyard.

The intention was to form a continuous weave of spaces, internal and external, which closely follow the contour of the land. Exposed windows have slatted timber shutters, which allow the façade to be protected in high winds. The siting and the language stem from the vernacular buildings in the area.

above
– seaward elevation
below
– verandah
– plan

Dix House
Howth, Co Dublin (1995-98)

This villa-type house sits on a sloping site with an oblique view of Howth harbour, Ireland's Eye and Lambay Island. The location is otherwise suburban, with an architecturally varied series of detached houses.

The house is split into two blocks, one jutting past the other to view the sea. The fracture locates the main entrance and the top-lit staircase, which connects the basement and intermediate levels with the roof-garden level. Howth stone is used to form a base, which contains a car port, utility room and guest bedrooms, and, together with stone retaining walls to the front of the site, 'grounds' the house into the land

above
– seaward elevation, with angled blocks atop stone base
below
– rear elevation, with deck
– entrance floor plan

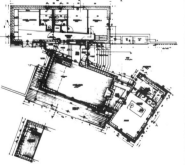

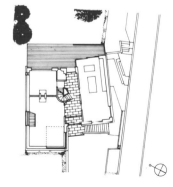

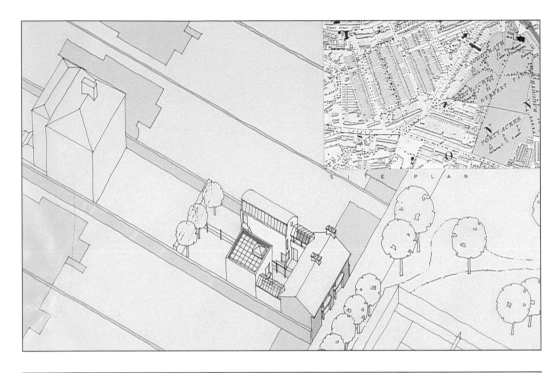

Boland and Kane Mews Houses
Clyde Lane, Dublin 4 (1990-92)

The site is located in the 19th-century inner suburbs of Dublin. The typological arrangement of these plots is that of the 'grand' house to the front, with the smaller-scale mews building to the rear. Clyde Lane is a one-sided, south-facing lane overlooking a public park. A mature hedge and cherry trees act as a natural screen between the main house and the mews. The brief was to convert and extend a stone mews into two independent living units – one for a businessman and the other for an artist.

The idea was to preserve the mews and place two 'pavilions' in the garden, making a distinct separation between the old and the new, and using two complementary forms: the cube, with its roof-garden, occupies the wider site; the long roof-lit studio for the artist occupies the narrower site.

Two archways are formed in the stone wall of the existing mews to allow cars onto the site. The archways, with living-room balconies overhead, form new 'front doors' – modern steel insets into the stone wall. The column is positioned to separate pedestrian from car access, and the gateways are splayed to form deep thresholds between public and private. One enters through this gateway into the space of the courtyard and the garden.

The sleeping area occupies the ground level of each mews, and the living and studio spaces are placed at the upper level to enjoy the view of the park and the light. The studio has a separate outdoor staircase and large doorway for moving large canvases.

– site axonometric and site plan
– section through courtyard

Hall House
Ranelagh, Dublin 6 (1997-99)

Located on a confined corner site, the programme requiring living rooms, study and three bedrooms is contained within a brick volume on Mountpleasant Avenue, and concealed behind a granite screen to Bessborough Parade.

In order to take advantage of the best light, the accommodation is stacked and pushed to the outer edges, creating a stepped void of courtyards and terraces related to the interior at each level. This relationship is reinforced by a concrete-frame, cross-hair structure embedded in the interior. The concrete columns are pulled to the outer edges, allowing the space of the terrace to penetrate the interior. The concrete beams hang low in the space because of the 8m span, and also to accentuate the horizontality of the plan.

The materials relate to the adjacent brick gable and the coursed granite rubble boundary walls and gables on the street.

– Mountpleasant Avenue / Bessborough
  Parade corner
– sections through raised courtyard
– ground, first and second-floor plans
– site plan
– (opposite) courtyard at night

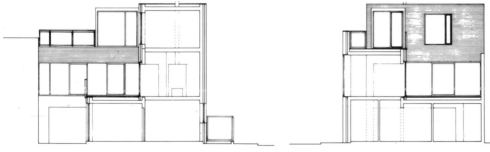

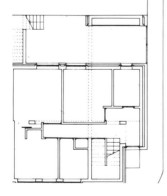

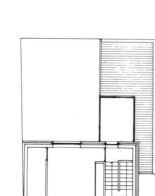

Naming Houses

A house is one of the few things people feel moved to name. Most commonly, they name them after places, often faraway in time or space, places of memory or dreams. When the house is the work of an architect, it usually takes the client's surname – partly out of pragmatism, but also as a memento of the relationships developed in its making. Occasionally, the client's name can become curiously appropriate, like in Schindler's How House, which seems to explore the 'how' of overlapping and telescoping spaces.

Houses have also been named for their particular constructional idea or typology. When this coincides with some sense of place, the name really sticks, like the Stone House by Herzog & de Meuron, set in a terraced landscape of drystone walls. In truth, this house owes as much to concrete as to stone, or might alternatively have been named for its enigmatic cruciform plan and section.

These houses belong to the same family as Grafton Architects' Hall House. This house is named after its owners, but other readings multiply at every turn: Brick House, Stone House, Stair House, Corner House, Diagonal House, Trestle House.

Further still, at one particular magnetic moment, beneath the unsupported crossing of the concrete trestles, the house offers the intriguing possibility of being named for something that is not even there: the House of the Lost Column. This absence is at the very point about which the internal and external spaces of the house pivot, relate and are drawn together.

Conor Moloney

The Eco House
(1995) (with Conservation Engineering)

We imagined a 'shell' for us to live in, a 'skin', an 'armour', which is precisely attuned to our needs, constructed with the minimum number of materials. Its intended quality emanates from its simple, modest, efficient form, its combination of raw materials and contemporary technology, hopefully making a place of pleasure, comfort and tranquillity for the restless, modern soul.

This energy-efficient prototypical apartment or house is 120m², for a family with two children. The unit is square in plan, with morning and evening courts. These courts act as microclimates, and form a layer of protection between the inside and outside world in terms of noise, pollution, wind, rain, sun, etc. The unit is organised around a massive central core, which acts as a central storage heater and which houses all the services, including a compost pipe and waste-collection wall fed directly from the kitchen.

The 'armour' or 'shell' is constructed in blue/black precast concrete, which consists of basalt lava aggregate with limestone chips. This is used at roof level, in the central core and on the south wall (where it is insulated by an outer layer of glass) to absorb and radiate heat. Natural concrete with inset fossils and salvaged rich materials are used internally, in the core and the south wall. Glass and timber screens connect the rooms to the courts. The movable external wall screens are constructed of bamboo, and provide protection from wind and sun. The movable roof screen is constructed of canvas or silk, stretched on carbon-fibre frames, like hang-gliders or wings.

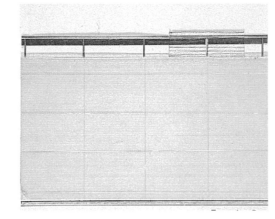
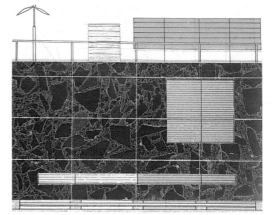

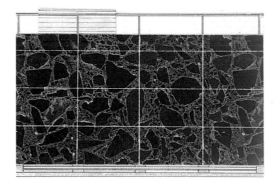
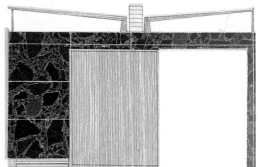

– south elevation – summer and winter
– north and east elevations
– ground and first-floor plans, and
  cross-section

Science of Materials Department
Trinity College, Dublin
(2nd stage competition entry, 1995)

A distinct characteristic of the campus at Trinity College is that, traditionally, long, narrow buildings are used to form the architectural quads and spaces. The spaces are experienced either as formal rooms or as informal, 'knuckle' in-between spaces, which link these external rooms.

The brief for this competition was to provide 10,000m² of flexible laboratory space with attendant offices.

Our initial idea was to use the 'narrow' block as 'fragments' or 'shards' of building strewn in a seemingly informal way on the floor of the campus. The project was also conceived as a splintered and split solid which responded to the colliding geometries and axes of campus and city, and allowed space and light to invade and filter between the parts. We were intrigued by ideas of interpreting space as energy released when matter and solids are split and fractured.

This fractured plan presents solid stone gables to the main campus, and these gables, together with the existing buildings, form the third side of a new formal square. In contrast, the transparency of the south walls visually unifies the separate buildings, so that there is a definite precinct for the science of materials department.

This transparent skin was thought about as a layered environmental filter controlling heat and light, and was inspired by the science theme of the competition and by the study of crystals, which have the capacity to polarise light and to rearrange light to suit their own structural patterns.

Section Looking West

On Grafton Architects

KENNETH FRAMPTON

> Opposed to the Regionalism of Restriction is another type of regionalism: the Regionalism of Liberation. This is the manifestation of a region that is *especially in tune with the emerging thought of the time*. We call such a manifestation 'regional' *only because it has not yet emerged elsewhere*. It is the genius of this region to be more than ordinarily aware and more than ordinarily free. Its virtue is that its manifestation has *significance for the world outside itself*. To express this regionalism architecturally it is necessary that there be building – preferably a lot of building – at one time. Only so can the expression be sufficiently general, sufficiently varied, sufficiently forceful to capture people's imaginations and provide a friendly climate long enough for a new school of design to develop.
> — Harwell Hamilton Harris, 1954

It has become increasingly clear that one of the advantages of the media age is we can no longer distinguish in absolute terms between the culture of the centre and culture of the periphery, and that at least, as far as architecture is concerned, quality work is emerging all over the world, despite the proliferation of commodified production in every field. This paradox is as true of Ireland today as of anywhere, perhaps even more true here than in other places. One is aware of a local resurgence, reinforced by EU money and by other equally invisible factors; hence, the seeming prosperity of the country and an enviable critical approach to the transformation of reality that has characterised the best of Irish architecture over the past decade. 'The flag is in the breeze', as Louis Sullivan once said of Chicago in an equally propitious moment. This is surely one way in which culture may be made, by penetrating into the grain of the place in every sense of the word and by cultivating societal desire, without which, little of substance can be achieved, for without the will of the client, nothing is possible. One recalls Rilke's evocative lines: 'It wasn't yet they fed it with the feeling that it might exist.' And while one cannot afford to be sanguine about the ambiguities of provinciality, this is fairly the mode in which one has to interpret the work of Grafton Architects, for what has their effort been to date if not an attempt to create a provincial culture of architecture at the highest level?

As one looks at their first work for Trinity College – their extension to the Department of Mechanical Engineering – one is reminded of Mario Botta's slogan, 'building the site', for here one is placed before a sophisticated microcosm built at the back of an eclectic nineteenth-century pile and looking to the future as much as to the green heart of the campus that it can barely reach. In fact, we may say that it is an object lesson in how to build behind something and make it feel like a 'front'. The trick seems to be turned in this instance by the rotation of a cube that, faced in black basalt, stands in front of the lugubrious Parson's Building, and resuscitates it – in sum, a rationalist work standing on a granite base, and hence, by definition, sympathetic to the classical tradition of the campus and yet, at the same time, emanating modern energy. As far as its rationalist antecedents are concerned, one notes that it is closer to Spanish rather than Italian sources, to Alessandro de la Sota, say, rather than Terragni. From this, there follows the laconic character of its minimalist detailing, the horizontal fenestration and outriding louvres that face the academic offices and which serve perceptually to detach the cube from the basement workshop, faced in sand-blasted granite. In the last analysis, it is the double-height volume of the cube itself, with its asymmetric fenestration of unusual size and proportion, that throws one off as to the scale of the work. The fact that the building seems smaller than it is

seems to accelerate its illusion of gyration. All of this is consummated by the sensitive handling of the materials and by the optimistic way in which the ramped staircase approach affords access to the Parson's Building, while serving to ground the extension at the same time. There is a touch of Alvar Aalto here, most evident, perhaps, in the stepped, grassy bank adjacent to the existing lime trees and in the canted workshop rooflights.

Since this triumph, the architects have been invited to confront a new challenge, namely to build (both literally and metaphorically) within the random 'shards' of time with the intention of realising an organic whole. This, I take, is their second work for Trinity, a competition entry for the Science of Materials Department, which seems, at first glance, to be a tour de force in reconstructed

'deconstruction'. On closer inspection, however, one discovers that the 'shards' are more physical than temporal. They have largely arisen from contingent causes: in the first instance, the long, narrow buildings of the Trinity campus; in the second, the interplay between the orthogonal grid of the campus and the diagonal grain of the adjacent urban fabric (not to mention the railway). Last, but not least, the architects have introduced the crystalline metaphor for its capacity to allude directly to the origin of material. One notes how the intelligence departs at this juncture from the relatively straightforward tectonics of the mechanical engineering building to engage entirely different levels of discourse: in the first place, the ecological potential of built form; in the second, a sharp feeling for the intrinsic quality of material, for its properties, mode of production and use, together with a reflection upon the interface between nature and culture that architecture presupposes and applied science cannot entirely dispense with.

The second stage of the same competition makes all of this even more explicit, where the blocks are rendered in a mineral tint and where Kyanite crystals are evoked as a reference. The 'shards' have now assumed a smaller footprint, and the ratio of exterior to floor area now seems oddly inefficient, let alone the over-provision of escape stairs which presumably is the bureaucracy doing its subversive best. Otherwise, as in the first stage, efficiency in terms of energy conservation is the order of the day, and it would appear that the architects are committed to evolving a relatively unprecedented tectonic syntax based in large part on ecological constraints. Going beyond the blanket superimposition of photo-voltaic cells, which, together with obligatory double glazing used to be the standard response in this area, these buildings aspire to the poetics of the metabolic envelop to such a degree as to remind one of the work of such architects as Glen Murcutt, Renzo Piano and Thomas Herzog.

As from these environmental considerations, the strength of Grafton Architects' work clearly resides in their phenomenological sensibility, evident in their pointed quote from Primo Levi's *Periodic Table*.

> There are friendly metals and hostile metals. Tin is a friend because it forms an alloy with copper to give us bronze, the respectable material par excellence, notoriously perennial and well established, because it melts at a low temperature, almost like organic compounds, almost like us.

At both an environmental and a formal level, everything is altogether more resolved in Grafton Architects' entry for the Eco Logis international competition [illustrated below], in which they gained second prize. Here one understands immediately how the layered microclimate comes to be seasonally induced, how hollow-tubed, Techcrete black walls get to be heated and cooled through a modifiable combination of adjustable white louvres, low emissivity glass, and judiciously positioned doors, vents, flaps, water troughs and roller blinds. And while this is an ecological tour de force, it is also poetic and accessible work. One only wishes it could now be taken further (particularly with regard to the furnishing of the micro space, c.f. Eileen Gray) by being realised, preferably by the architects themselves for their own occupation, for this is the stuff out of which the modern movement was once made, the postulation of a canonical work demonstrating the possibility for a new way of life. This, surely, is Grafton Architects at their best, and one only wishes they would have the opportunity of applying the same criteria to low-rise, high-density housing in order to move towards the 'world as a garden', as Roland Rainer once put it when referring to China prior to the present global apocalypse.

Kenneth Frampton is Ware Professor of Architecture at Columbia University. He has written extensively, and his publications include *Modern Architecture: A Critical History* and *Studies in Tectonic Culture*.

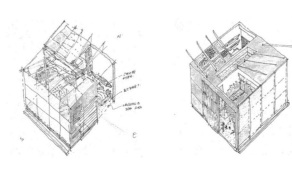

GRAFTON ARCHITECTS

Yvonne Farrell and Shelley McNamara worked independently in private practice in Dublin from 1976-78. They established Grafton Architects with Shay Cleary, Frank Hall and Tony Murphy in 1978. They were founder members of Group 91 Architects in 1991.

COLLABORATORS – Seamus Carr, Gerard Carty (associate), Eoin St John Downes, Miriam Dunn, Declan Fallon, Alastair Hall, Iseult Hall, John Barry Lowe, Esmonde O'Briain, Eilis O'Donnell, Rosie O'Grady, Lisa O'Regan, Philippe O'Sullivan (associate), Michael Pike, Emmett Scanlon, Gregg Smeaton, Tracey Staunton

YVONNE FARRELL

	Born in Tullamore, Co Offaly
1969-74	University College Dublin (BArch)
1974-75	Cross, Dixon, Gold, Jones, Sansom, London
1975-76	Cathal O'Neill & Associates, Dublin
1978-	Studio lecturer, School of Architecture, UCD
	Visiting critic, Architectural Association, London;
	Royal College of Art and Design, London;
	Cambridge; Kingston
1991-94	President, Architectural Graduates Association, UCD
1998-01	External examiner, Kingston University, England
	Fellow, Royal Institute of the Architects of Ireland

SHELLEY McNAMARA

1952	Born in Lisdoonvarna, Co Clare
1969-74	University College Dublin (BArch)
1974-75	Louis de Soissons Architects, London
1978-	Studio lecturer, School of Architecture, UCD
1990-93	Board member, Irish Museum of Modern Art, Dublin
1995-98	External examiner, Oxford Brookes University
	Fellow, Royal Institute of the Architects of Ireland

GERARD CARTY (associate)

1964	Born in Tullamore, Co Offaly
1987	DIT School of Architecture, Dublin (BArch Sc TCD)
1988	Tod Wakefield, London
1989	McGarry NíÉanaigh Architects, Drogheda
1990	Guillermo Vazquez Consuegra, Seville
1993-	Grafton Architects, Dublin
	Studio lecturer, DIT School of Architecture

PHILIPPE O'SULLIVAN (associate)

1966	Born in Cavan
1990	DIT School of Architecture, Dublin (BArch Sc TCD)
	Stewart and Sinnott, Dublin
1992	Grafton Architects, Dublin
1996-98	Lecturer in building technology, DIT Rathmines

SELECTED BUILDINGS AND PROJECTS

1998   DOCKLANDS HOUSING COMPETITION, Dublin
(with Architon Group Practice)

1997-99 NORTH KING ST APARTMENTS, Smithfield, Dublin 7
(HARP Project, RIAI limited competition, 1st prize)
HALL HOUSE, Ranelagh, Dublin 6
COLÁISTE EOIN AGUS COLÁISTE ÍOSAGÁIN,
Stillorgan, Co Dublin
CIVIC CENTRE, Dunshaughlin, Co Meath

1997-98 OFFICE BUILDING, Little Strand Street, Dublin 7

1996-99 SCREENING ROOM FOR CLARENCE PICTURES,
Denzille Lane, Merrion Square, Dublin 2
CELBRIDGE COMMUNITY SCHOOL, Co Kildare

1996-98 SCHOOL EXTENSION, Ard Scoil Eanna, Crumlin,
Dublin 12

1996-97 GARDEN ROOM, Merrion Square, Dublin 2
(AAI Award, 1998)

1996   MEWS HOUSES, Clyde Lane, Dublin 4

1995-99 OUR LADY'S SECONDARY SCHOOL,
Castleblaney, Co Monaghan

1995-98 DIX HOUSE, Howth, Co Dublin
MARA HOLIDAY HOUSE, Kinvara, Co Galway
GILL HOLIDAY HOUSE, Westport, Co Mayo
MOTORWAY BRIDGE, Balbriggan, Co Dublin
(with Roughan & O'Donovan Engineers)

1995   SCIENCE OF MATERIALS DEPT, Trinity College Dublin
(RIAI limited competition, second-stage entry)
ECO HOUSE, Parc la Villette, Paris
(Eco Logis international competition, 2nd prize)

1994-96 DEPT OF MECHANICAL AND MANUFACTURING
ENGINEERING, Trinity College Dublin
(AAI Award, 1997; RIAI Award, 1997)
CO-OPERATIVE HOUSING, South Earl St, Dublin 7
(Group 91 / Grafton Architects)

1994-95 MOTORWAY BRIDGE, Bray, Co Wicklow
(with Roughan & O'Donovan) (AAI Award, 1995)

1993-95 GRAY AND O'CONNELL HOUSE, Doolin, Co Clare
(AAI Award, 1995)

1992-96 TEMPLE BAR SQUARE, Dublin 2
(Group 91 / Grafton Architects)

(RIAI Award, 1997; Special Mention, AAI Awards 1997)

1991-96 TEMPLE BAR FRAMEWORK PLAN
(Group 91) (RIAI limited competition, 1st prize)

1990-92 BOLAND AND KANE MEWS HOUSES, Clyde Lane,
Dublin 4 (AAI Award, 1993)

1989-92 ST PAUL'S SECONDARY SCHOOL, Oughterard,
Co Galway (Special Mention, AAI Awards 1993)

1988-90* OFFICE BUILDING, Ormond Quay, Dublin 7
(Special Mention, AAI Awards 1990)

1988   CANOE CLUB, Chapelizod, Co Dublin

1985-86 SCHOOL EXTENSION, Killaloe, Co Clare
(with Dowling Architects)

1983-88* COMMUNITY SCHOOL, Killaloe, Co Clare
(with Dowling Architects)

1980-83* SCHOOL EXTENSION, Lisdoonvarna, Co Clare

1979-80* GRAPHIC ART STUDIO, Clyde Lane, Dublin 4

1978-80* OUTDOOR PURSUITS CENTRE, The Burren, Co Clare
        * designed with Tony Murphy

SELECTED EXHIBITIONS

1999   *Grafton Architects*, Architecture Centre, Dublin

1998   *Competitions*, Architecture Centre, Dublin

1997-98 *20th Century Architecture: Ireland*, Deutsches
Architektur-Museum, Frankfurt; RIBA, London;
RHA Gallagher Gallery, Dublin

1996   *The Power of an Idea*, Temple Bar, Dublin
Building on the Edge of Europe
(l'Imaginaire Irlandais), Maison d'Architecture, Paris
Eco Logis, Parc la Villette, Paris

1991   *Making a Modern Street* (Group 91),
Riverrun Gallery, Dublin; Architektur Forum, Zürich;
Irish Museum of Modern Art, Dublin

1988   *Architecture Publiques*, Palais de Chaillot, Paris

1979   *Traditions and Directions* (Sense of Ireland), London

GRAFTON ARCHITECTS, 97 Grafton Street, Dublin 2
tel: +353 (0)1 6713365 / fax: 6713178
e-mail: graftonarchitects@indigo.ie

GANDON EDITIONS

Gandon Editions is the leading producer of books on Irish art and architecture.

Gandon Editions was established in 1983 and was named after the architect James Gandon (1743-1823), as the initial focus was on architecture titles. In the 1980s, we published books on international architects Aldo Rossi and Josef Paul Kleihues (1983), and *A Lost Tradition – The Nature of Architecture in Ireland* by McCullough and Mulvin (1987). We also established the *New Irish Architecture* (AAI Awards) series, now in its fifteenth year.

We now produce 20 to 25 art and architecture titles per year, both under the Gandon imprint and on behalf of a wide range of art and architectural institutions in Ireland. We have produced over 200 titles to date.

Gandon books are available from good bookshops in Ireland and abroad, or direct from:

GANDON EDITIONS
Oysterhaven, Kinsale, Co Cork, Ireland

tel	+353 (0)21-770830
fax	+353 (0)21-770755
e-mail	gandon@eircom.net
web-site	www.gandon-editions.com

PROFILES

In 1996, Gandon Editions launched PROFILES – a series of medium-format books on contemporary Irish artists. In 1997, we launched a companion series on contemporary Irish architects. Both series are edited and designed by John O'Regan.

Each volume in the PROFILES series carries two major texts – an essay and an interview with the artist / architect – and is heavily illustrated in colour. They are of a standard design, with 48 or 60 pages in a 23 cm square format, and retail at £7.50 paperback.

To date, we have published eleven titles in the art series and three in the architecture series.

ARCHITECTURE PROFILES

already published

Profile 1 – O'DONNELL AND TUOMEY
interview by Kester Rattenbury; texts by Hugh Campbell, Kevin Kieran, Robert Maxwell, Wilfried Wang, Williams & Tsien
ISBN 0946641 986   Gandon Editions, 1997

Profile 2 – McGARRY NíÉANAIGH
essay by Raymund Ryan
interview by Dermot Boyd
ISBN 0946641 994   Gandon Editions, 1997

Profile 3 – GRAFTON ARCHITECTS
essays by Hugh Campbell, Kenneth Frampton, Elizabeth Hatz
interview by Raymund Ryan
ISBN 0946846 049   Gandon Editions, 1999

titles in preparation

SHAY CLEARY ARCHITECTS
(Spring 2000)

McCULLOUGH MULVIN
(Spring 2000)

to be continued ...